# Summer

by
Emilie Dufresne

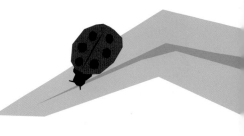

# BookLife
## PUBLISHING

©2018
BookLife Publishing
King's Lynn
Norfolk PE30 4LS

All rights reserved.
Printed in Malaysia.

A catalogue record for this book is available from the British Library.

**ISBN:** 978-1-78637-404-2

**Written by:**
Emilie Dufresne

**Edited by:**
Kirsty Holmes

**Designed & Illustrated by:**
Danielle Jones

All facts, statistics, web addresses and URLs in this book were verified as valid and accurate at time of writing. No responsibility for any changes to external websites or references can be accepted by either the author or publisher.

# IMAGE CREDITS

Cover – Kamira. 4 – Tatyana Vyc. 5 – TY Lim. 6 – vvvita. 7 – Samuel Borges Photography. 8 – Anna Nahabed. 10 – AKKHARAT JARUSILAWONG. 11 – Agnes Kantaruk. 12 – windmoon. 14 – SherSor. 15 – gpointstudio 16 – MNStudio. 18 – Lucian Coman. 19 – Szasz-Fabian Jozsef. 20 – Pakhnyushchy. 22–23 – mandritoiu. Illustrations by Danielle Jones. Images are courtesy of Shutterstock.com. With thanks to Getty Images, Thinkstock Photo and iStockphoto.

# CONTENTS

Words that look like <u>this</u> can be found in the glossary on page 24.

# It's Summer!

The sun is shining. The weather is hot.
It must be… summer!

Summer is a season of the year. Seasons change when the weather changes. Every season is different.

Summer

Autumn

Spring

Winter

# Summer
## Weather

In summer, the weather is warm.
If we are lucky the sun shines in the sky!

Summer is the season when the days are longest.

THAT MEANS MORE TIME FOR PLAYING!

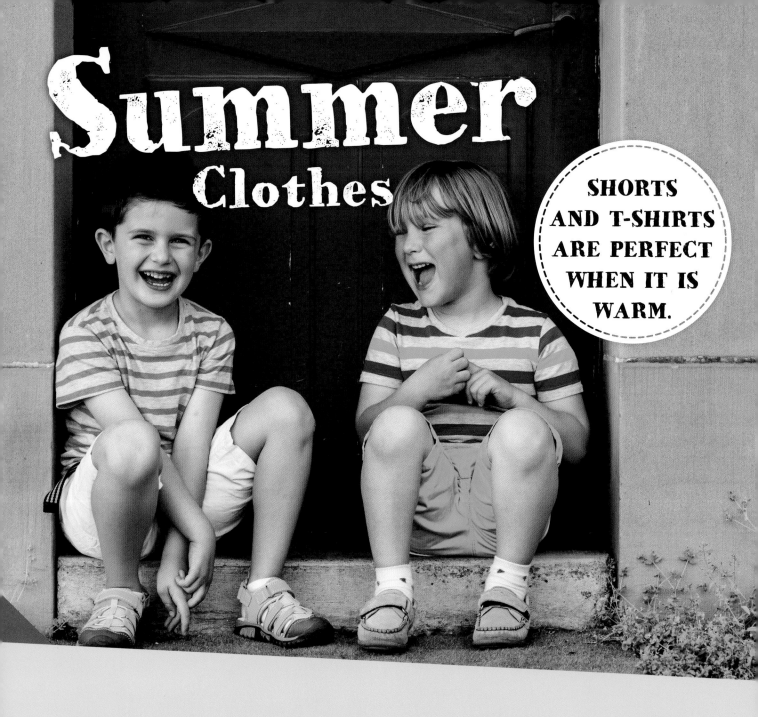

# Summer
## Clothes

When it is warm we do not need lots of clothes.

We need to make sure our bodies are protected in the sunshine.

Sun Cream

Hat

Sunglasses

# Summer
## Festivals and Celebrations

Nebuta Matsuri is a Japanese summer festival. There are lots of colourful <u>floats</u>.

In Poland, they celebrate the Wianki Festival.
Wianki means <u>wreaths</u>.

PEOPLE
MAKE
WREATHES
TO FLOAT
ON RIVERS.

THE BOATS ARE MADE TO LOOK LIKE DRAGONS!

The Dragon Boat Festival happens in China. People race long, thin boats.

Zongzi is <u>traditionally</u> eaten at the Dragon Boat Festival.

INSIDE THE BAMBOO LEAF IS STICKY RICE. ZONGZI CAN BE SWEET OR <u>SAVOURY</u>!

Bamboo Leaf

Sticky Rice

Sweet or Savoury Fillings

# Summer
## Food

Strawberries

Watermelon

WHAT FRUITS HAVE YOU TRIED?

Passion Fruit

Lots of colourful fruits are <u>in season</u> in summer.

When it is hot, it is nice to eat and drink cold things.

ICE CREAM IS A GREAT WAY TO KEEP COOL IN SUMMER!

# Summer
## Play

WATER FIGHTS HELP US TO COOL DOWN.

It is fun to have a water fight in the summer.

16

In summer it is nice to go on picnics.
People can eat outside and play games.

HAVE
YOU EVER
BEEN ON
A PICNIC?

# Plants in Summer

DO NOT FORGET TO WATER YOUR PLANTS OR THEY WILL DRY OUT!

Plants need sunlight to grow. That means plants do lots of growing in summer.

18

Fruits and vegetables are ready to eat in summer. When they are ready we can pick them!

HAVE YOU EVER PICKED FRUIT?

19

# Animals in Summer

Bees are their most active in the summer. They are busy collecting pollen and nectar. They use the nectar to make honey.

Some animals <u>moult</u> at the beginning of summer.
Animals like cats, rabbits and dogs shed fur.

THEIR COATS
GET THINNER IN
SUMMER SO THAT
THEY AREN'T
TOO HOT!

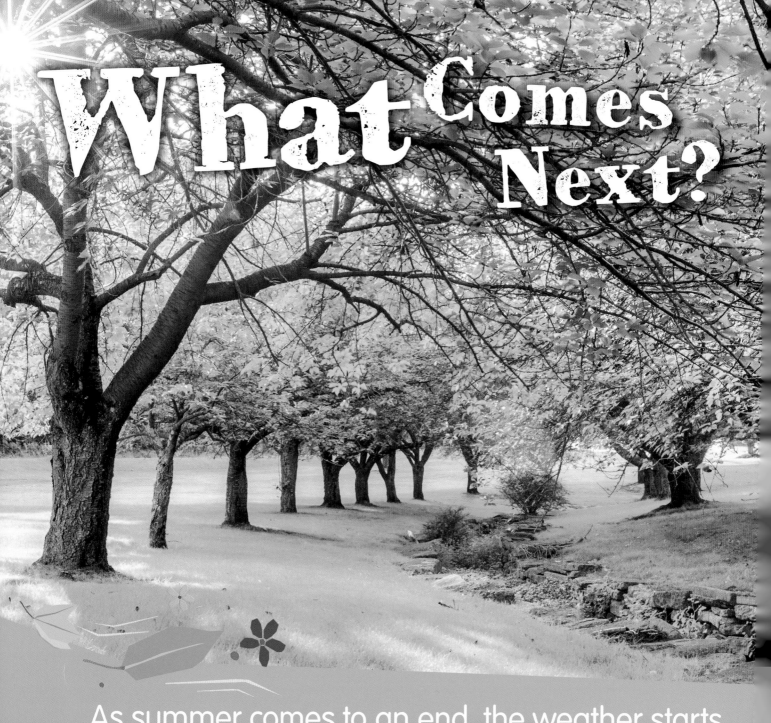

# What Comes Next?

As summer comes to an end, the weather starts to get colder. The days start to get shorter.

Summer is becoming… autumn!

23

# GLOSSARY

**floats**         a moving platform with decorations that are usually used in parades

**in season**      when a plant grows best

**moult**        when an animal loses hair, feathers or skin to make way for new growth

**savoury**     food that is salty or spicy, but not sweet

**traditionally**  very old behaviours and beliefs

**wreaths**     a ring-shaped arrangement of flowers and leaves

# INDEX

24